© Macmillan Publishers Limited, 1984
All rights reserved. No part of this publication may be reproduced or transmitted, in any form or by any means, without permission.

Printed in Hong Kong

ISBN 0 333 373049

First published in 1984 by
Macmillan Children's Books,
a division of Macmillan Publishers Limited,
4, Little Essex Street, London WC2R 3LF
and Basingstoke

Associated companies in
New York, Toronto, Dublin,
Melbourne, Johannesburg and Delhi

Designer
Julian Holland

Picture researcher
Stella Martin

Artists
Jim Marks
Sarah Pooley

Editors
Miranda Smith
Lynne Williams

Photocredits:
AGA Infrared Systems Ltd
Apple Computers (UK) Ltd
Association of Universities for Research in Astronomy, Inc.
The Kitt Peak National Observatory
Biofotos
J Allan Cash Ltd
Bruce Coleman Ltd
Jesse Davis
Electrolux Ltd
Haags Gemeentemuseum
Honeywell Control Systems
Eric and David Hosking
Hughes Aircraft Company
Lucasfilm Ltd
Stella Martin
NASA
Natural History Photographic Agency
Natural Science Photos
Picturepoint Ltd
Polaroid (UK) Ltd
Premaphotos Wildlife
Science Photo Library
Servis Domestic Appliances Ltd
Mark Shearman
Spectrum Colour Library
Thorn EMI Ferguson
John Watney
ZEFA

The Senses

Graham Storrs

Contents

What are senses?	4
What is sensed?	7
The human eye	10
Fooling the eye	13
Sight in other creatures	16
Machines with vision	19
Touch	22
Hearing	25
Smell	28
Taste	31
Position sense	34
Senses adapted for protection	37
Senses adapted for navigation	40
Machine senses in navigation	43
Senses for communication	46
Extending human senses	49
Machine senses for survival	52
Five other senses	55
Beyond human senses	58
Some useful machines	61
Index	65

◁ A male elk.

What are senses?

▽ It is the brain's job to make sense of the thousands of signals it receives all the time. For each sense there is a special area of the brain which interprets its messages.

The senses are our window onto the world. Only through them can we know what is going on inside or outside our own bodies.

Our senses collect information about the world and pass it on to the brain which puts it all together to form a complete 'picture' of what is going on. The human brain is made up of about 10,000,000,000 nerve cells.

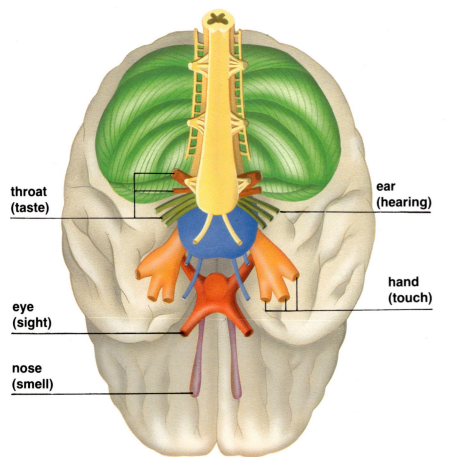

throat (taste)
ear (hearing)
hand (touch)
eye (sight)
nose (smell)

Hearing
△ The part of the ear you see is just a tube which leads sound into the inner ear or 'ear drum' where it is detected. Sound is passed to the inner ear by tiny bones called ossicles. These pass the sound to a coiled tube containing the vibration-sensitive cells.

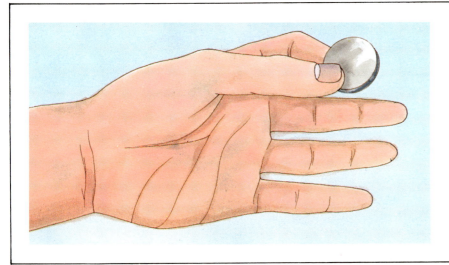

Touch
◁ Our sense of touch relies on nerve cells in the skin. Whenever these cells are moved because something touches the skin, they send a message to the brain. We include a lot of other senses in with our sense of touch, such as pain, heat and cold. All these have special receptors in the skin.

Smell
◁ When we can smell something we are detecting chemicals in the air. When we sniff, these chemicals are drawn past sensitive cells at the back of the nose where they give rise to signals which travel up to the brain. Each smell has its own particular signal which the brain recognizes.

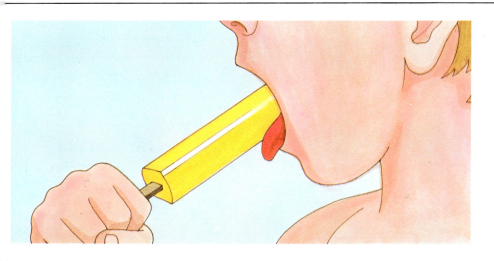

Taste
◁ The tongue is sensitive to only four different tastes; sweet, salt, bitter, and sour. Each taste is detected on a different part of the tongue. The four basic tastes are very important ones. Sweet and salt normally mean that the food is good to eat; bitter and sour normally mean it is not.

Sight
◁ Eyes are hollow balls full of clear liquid. Light goes in through a hole at the front called the pupil. Light is focused by a lens onto the retina at the back of the eye, where the light-sensitive nerve cells are. The signals from the retina pass along the optic nerve to reach the brain.

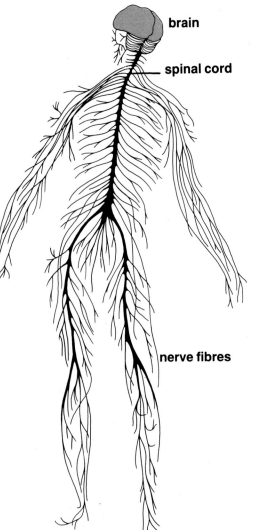

The senses are a set of millions of nerve endings of different kinds grouped together into the various sense organs (such as the eyes and the nose). Here they can feel the world around them. Their information is passed along a complex channel of nerve fibres, through the spinal cord, and into the brain. This makes an elaborate web of nerves, with the brain at the centre and the senses around the outside.

IMPORTANT

Boiler Cleaning
Further to the instructions contained in the booklet, flushing of the boiler should be continued until all trace of soldering deposits are removed—several fillings of hot water may be necessary.

Running
Water consumption may be excessive during initial running due to priming. The water level must be checked carefully and if the water level falls to the 'MIN' mark on the sight glass, the burner must be removed immediately. It is recommended that distilled water be used in hard water areas.

WICHTIG

Reinigen des Kessels
Über die in der Bedienungsanleitung hierzu enthaltenen Maßnahmen hinaus den Kessel so lange ausspülen, bis alle Spuren von Lötablagerungen entfernt sind—mehrere Füllungen mit heißem Wasser können erforderlich sein.

Fahrbetrieb
Beim ersten Lauf kann der Wasserverbrauch höher als normal sein, da sich die Leitungen füllen. Der Wasserstand muß daher sorgfältig beobachtet werden: Falls er auf die 'MIN'-Markierung am Schauglas fällt, sofort den Brenner entfernen.

△ Here are some instructions in two languages. Although you may only understand one, both say the same thing. The messages your senses send to the brain are in a code which only it can translate. Each sense has its own code, but the brain works to decipher them all.

△ Your senses send their messages to the brain along nerve fibres. Some of these have to be very long. The brain and its nerve fibres form the nervous system. This looks like a wiring diagram if drawn without the rest of the body.

▷ Computers have many extra devices which act like senses, sending the computer coded messages about the world outside. Like us, computers have a wide variety of senses.

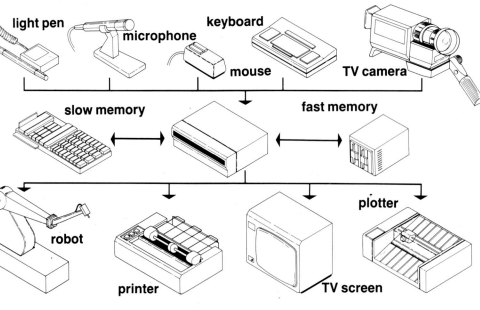

What is sensed?

Our senses are very particular about what kinds of stimulation they will respond to. Each of them prefers its own special type of stimulus.

We can put the kinds of things we can sense into three groups; chemicals (like tastes and smells), movements and vibrations (such as touch and sound), and radiations (such as light and heat).

△ Balance, touch and hearing are all mechanical senses. They each depend on some movement of the nerve cells to trigger the signals which let the brain know what is happening. The balance of a dancer such as these depends on sensing movements in the muscles, the joints and in the inner ears. Touch needs movements of the skin and hearing depends on very small movements caused by sound waves in the air.

Experiment!

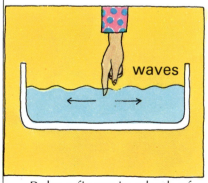

Poke a finger in a bath of water and waves will move out from it. The waves will

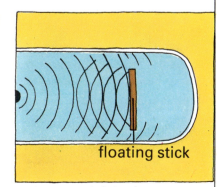

move a stick in the water just as sound waves move your ear drum.

The simplest chemical sense is known as the Common Chemical Sense and is an irritation felt by the eyes, nose, mouth and other places when certain chemicals are around, such as ammonia and acid fumes. It is this sense which causes so much trouble when you peel an onion!

Taste and smell are by far our most elaborate chemical senses and, between them, are sensitive to thousands of different chemicals.

Hearing, touch and the position senses are all mechanical senses – they respond to movement and vibration.

Sound is channelled by our ears into the inner ear where it passes along a set of tiny bones to vibrate a thin membrane. This is stretched like a drumskin across the end of a narrow, coiled tube. This tube contains the thousands of nerve cells which respond to sound.

◁ Here is a Canadian otter enjoying a meal. The food he is eating, like all food, is made of chemicals. These chemicals stimulate his senses of taste and smell. The smell of food actually helps us to eat and digest it by triggering the production of extra saliva and the flow of digestive juices in the stomach.

Extra saliva not only helps digest food, but it helps us to taste it as well, because it keeps the mouth wet. This is important because taste depends upon chemicals in the food being dissolved in the saliva surrounding your taste buds.

The taste buds are the sites of the nerve endings in your tongue and are sensitive only to dissolved chemicals. If your tongue was dry, you would not be able to taste dry foods.

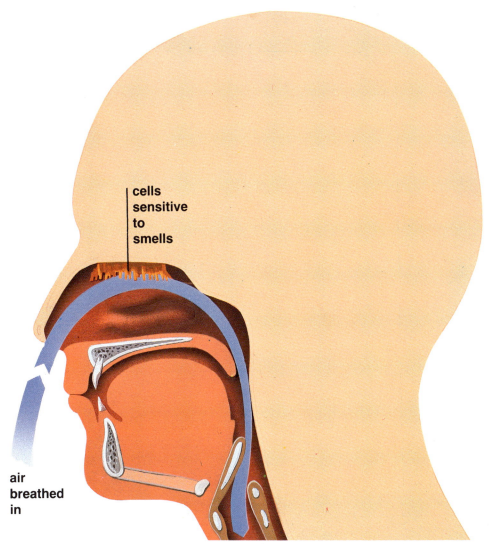

In our skin there are a number of different types of nerve cell which respond to different types of movement. Some, which look like tiny onions, are most sensitive to pressure, while others are more sensitive to movements of the skin. Some wrap themselves around the roots of hairs so that they can detect any movement of the hair.

Our position sense depends on nerve endings in muscles and tendons which send signals when they are stretched. It also uses the cells in joints which respond to movements. Finally it makes use of the hair-like cells in our inner ear which move as we move our heads or when we change position.

Radiation
Heat and light are kinds of radiation. Other kinds of radiation are radio waves and nuclear radiation. Some kinds of radiation can be felt by our senses and some cannot. We cannot feel radio waves even though the air is constantly full of them, but we can feel light with our eyes and heat with our skin.

△ Taste and smell are chemical senses. They rely on various chemicals in our mouths or noses to give rise to all the varied sensations we feel.

Chemicals are made up of millions and millions of atoms and molecules. When these molecules touch the surface of the cells in our nose or mouth, those cells send their signals to the brain. Different molecules cause different signals to be sent and the brain understands these as different tastes or smells.

The human eye

The most important sense we have is our eyesight. To convince yourself of this, ask a friend to blindfold you and then try to carry on as you normally would. Because of your eyesight you can move about easily, recognize people and things, read and write, play sports and games and do your work.

We see because our eyes take the light coming from objects around us and convert it into signals which our brains work on. There are about a million nerve cells in each of our eyes and millions more in our brains which do the work of turning light into the images we see.

Our eyes are very good at what they do. They can see extremely fine detail and can tell many different colours apart. Because they work together when they look at things, they give us information about depth and distance by allowing the brain to compare the slightly different images from each eye.

▽ This is a picture of the inside of a human eye. Most other mammals, reptiles, fish and birds have eyes that work in a very similar way. At the back of our eyes is a layer of very sensitive cells called the retina. Light coming from things in the world outside is focused by the lens at the front of the eye to form an image on the retina. The cells in the retina then send messages about this image along the optic nerve to the brain.

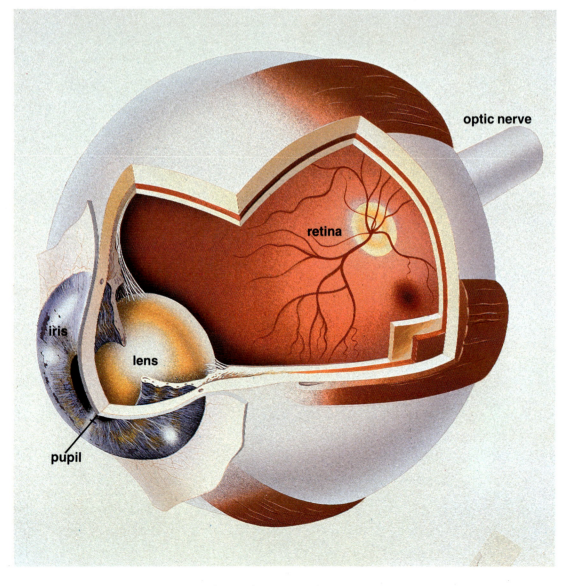

The eye and its pupils

The amount of light that enters the eye is controlled by the iris. This is a muscle at the front of the eye which simply opens or closes a small hole called the pupil. If it is dark, the pupil will be large (*left*) so as to let in more light. If it is bright the pupil will be small (*right*). Pupil size can also change quite noticeably with your mood.

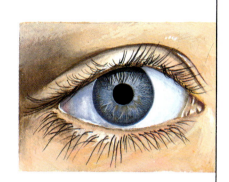

How our eyes work

Your eyes are ball-shaped and are about the size of golf-balls. The white part of your eye is a tough outer skin which protects the delicate nerves inside. The eye is filled with a clear liquid and the lens of the eye is made of a clear jelly-like substance.

The lens is focused by tiny muscles which pull it into the right shape. In front of the lens is a tough layer of clear skin called the cornea. This is very sensitive to being touched. It is kept clear of dust and dirt by the eyelids which are constantly blinking to wipe the surface of the eye clean.

Muscles fixed to the outside of each eyeball turn the eye from side to side and up and down. The brain makes sure that both eyes are always pointing in the same direction.

The optic nerve

All the nerve cells in the retina send their signals through a thick bundle of nerve fibres called the optic nerve. This carries the signals to a large area at the back of the brain where most of the work of interpreting them goes on. Where the optic nerve joins the retina you have a blind spot on each eye. You do not notice your blind spots because your brain 'smooths over' the missing piece of the image.

Correcting eye-sight

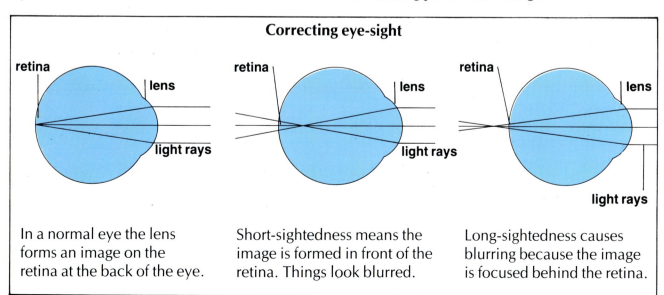

In a normal eye the lens forms an image on the retina at the back of the eye.

Short-sightedness means the image is formed in front of the retina. Things look blurred.

Long-sightedness causes blurring because the image is focused behind the retina.

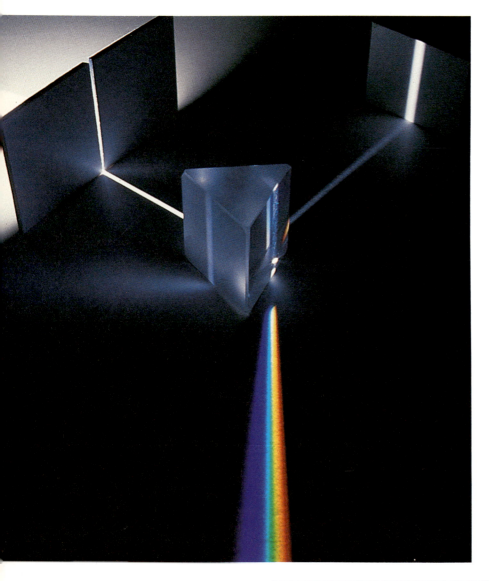

△ The retina is made up of cells called rods and cones. Cones are used to see colours but need lots of light. Rods cannot detect colour but are light-sensitive. At night we may still be able to see – but only in black and white.

△ White light is a mixture of coloured light. It can be split up again into its different colours using a prism like this.

When light falls on the retina, special colour-detecting cells called cones send signals to the brain. The cones are sensitive to red, green and blue light. They send their red, green and blue signals up to the brain where they are mixed again so that we are able to see the original colour.

Experiment!

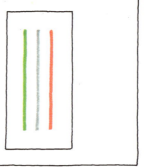

Look at this pattern through pieces of clear red and green plastic. The

differences in what our two eyes see give the impression of depth.

Fooling the eye

Optical illusions are deliberate attempts to fool the eye. They show us a lot about how the eye works. But it is not only people who make a living out of fooling the eye. Many animals also use their own colouring or patterning or even the shape of their bodies to fool the eyes of predators or prey.

Many are able to use protective colouring or camouflage to make themselves blend in with their surroundings. The stick insect, which can sometimes be seen in hedges, is coloured like a twig and has a body and legs which look very like the twigs it sits on. The chameleon is famous for its ability to change the colour of its skin to the colour of its background. The eye of an enemy must not be able to tell an animal from its background, so patches of colour, spots and stripes which break up its outline all make an animal harder to see.

▽ To understand what we see when we look at a picture, we use a wide range of clues. These include perspective, texture, and whether objects overlap each other. It is part of an artist's craft to make use of these clues to fool the eye into believing that what he has painted is not just flat. The cars in this picture are seen against a painted background, but to us it looks real.

◁ Normally, people can easily make sense of what they see. Our eyes and brain work very well together to understand what we are looking at in the real world, but when we come to look at pictures the eye can easily be fooled.

This is because our brain automatically assumes certain things about what the eye is seeing. For instance, if a picture shows on object covering part of another, the brain will assume that the first object is nearer than the second.

Follow the staircase in this picture with your eyes and see where it leads you!

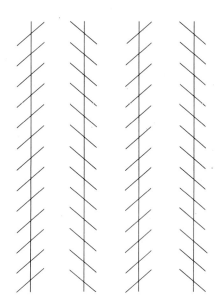

△ The vertical lines in this picture are parallel, but they do not look it! Scientists do not know how these and many other illusions work.

◁ Here is a colour negative picture of a bowl of fruit. Stare at it for 20 seconds without moving your eyes and then look at a white wall. You will see an image of the fruit in its true colours. This effect is due to the chemicals in your eyes which enable you to see colour.

Light reacts with these chemicals to send signals to the brain, but this uses up the chemicals and your eye has to make more.

The chemical which reacts to green light is used up when you look at a green picture. If you then look at a white wall (which has all the colours mixed together) your eye is not very sensitive to green. The other colours will seem stronger and you will see red or orange.

△ Which is the longer line, X or Y? Actually they are both the same but your eyes tell you the vertical line is the longer.

Experiment!

Make a star shape on a piece of paper and stand a mirror behind it.

Watch your hand in the mirror and try to trace the shape with a pencil.

Sight in other creatures

Our own eyesight is complicated and fascinating, but it is by no means the end of the story of the sense of sight. Almost all animals have some kind of sensitivity to light and the enormous number of animals which have eyesight of one kind or another shows us the great importance of this sense. Even plants are sensitive to light and will turn their leaves to face the sunlight.

People are fortunate in having good colour vision since this is very rare among mammals. Birds, reptiles and even fish are usually sensitive to colour. Some animals, such as insects, can even see colours which people cannot.

A wide range of eyesight

It may surprise you to hear how very similar other animals' eyes are to our own. Creatures such as octopusses and snakes which seem quite different to us have eyes which are similar to ours. Yet some animals, such as lobsters and butterflies, have eyes which work in a very different way. And the 'eyes' of some creatures, the earthworm for example, may only be patches of light-sensitive skin.

◁ This buzzard, like most birds, has extremely good eyesight and can see fine details which we would be unable to pick out.

With good eyesight a person should be able to see a gap of only a millimetre from over three metres away. The buzzard and other birds of prey could stand twice as far away and still see it. This means they can fly high in the air and spot tiny creatures, such as mice, far below them.

Some animals, like cats, are long-sighted and have trouble seeing things which are too close. Most insects are short-sighted and cannot see for more than a few centimetres.

▷ Like most insects the housefly has eyes which are made up of thousands of tiny lenses. They are called compound eyes. On male flies, the eyes can meet in the middle and cover the whole head. Spiders, which also have compound eyes, can often have as many as eight eyes set in a ring around their heads.

Each lens in a compound eye is part of a very simple but complete eye. Each simple eye may have only eight nerve cells in it (our own eyes have a million nerve cells!). The lens cannot focus, so flies can only see clearly at very close range.

There are many ways in which the sense of sight can be used to help animals survive. Some small creatures, such as earthworms and woodlice, use their crude sense of light and dark to help them to avoid the light where predators such as birds and frogs, can find them and where their moist skins might dry up.

Sight and its uses

Other animals have more complex uses for their more developed sense of sight. Insects do not see clearly except at close distances, but their eyesight helps them to find food and to avoid danger. Bees and wasps are able to see colour and are attracted by the bright displays of blossom and flowers which are made by many plants. Their eyes are sensitive to the movements of approaching predators and so give them warning of danger.

Insects also use their eyesight in communicating with other insects. The glowing tail of the glow-worm can tell other glow-worms where he is. The figure-of-eight dance of the honey bee tells the other bees in which direction and how far away it is to the food she has found.

Other groups

When we look at other groups, we find that they also use their eyesight for locating food, avoiding dangers and communicating. However, these animals often rely on vision a lot more than earthworms and woodlice. They also find new uses for vision.

Moving about requires vision, but reaching and grasping need the guidance of vision too. Tool-using animals, such as people or monkeys who throw stones or use sticks to probe for insects, need their eyesight to help identify the tool, to position it in their grasp and to adjust its position as they work with it. When it is highly developed, eyesight can be used to recognize other animals, some of which might be predators, and to recognize places. It can therefore help the animal find food and shelter.

◁ Judging distances can be important. Monkeys spend much of their time in trees and need to be very accurate as they move among the branches. Having their eyes set at the front of their heads makes this easier for them.

Compare this baboon's eyes to the buzzard's. On land, grazing animals have eyes at the sides of their head while hunters have their eyes at the front.

▷ Some animals have eyes which are especially adapted to their needs.

The frog in this picture, like other frogs, has eyes which are very good at detecting small moving black objects – which is very handy if you are trying to catch flies to eat!

Machines with vision

Although human vision is extremely good when it is compared with sight in certain other animals, people have found it lacking in several ways. The spectrum of visible light (*page 12*) is only a part of the whole range of colours to be seen and the distances at which we can see clear detail have often seemed far too short.

People have tried to overcome these shortcomings by developing special machines. These can see kinds of light and amounts of detail that we cannot and they can interpret what they are seeing well enough to produce images for us, so that we can see with our own eyes.

Yet it could be even more useful if our machines could understand what they are seeing well enough to be able to use a sense of sight for themselves. Then our machines would be able to do far more, such as driving tractors, cleaning houses and mining minerals, than they can now.

Robots

A variety of robot vision systems has been built to help robots which work in industry but these are still very, very crude compared to our own. The problem is that it takes an extremely clever brain to interpret the messages that an eye sends to it. Even the brains of frogs and spiders are more intelligent in this respect than the computer 'brains' that our robots have.

▷ This photograph is of San Francisco Bay and it was taken from space. A special camera was used which records infra-red light which our own eyes are unable to see. A computer was used to add the colours to show where the infra-red light was strongest. This kind of picture can tell scientists a lot about what is happening on the ground.

Fields with different kinds of crop growing in them reflect different amounts of infra-red light and will appear in different colours. This is also true for different kinds of soil and rock.

◁ It is still not possible to build machines, like these from a film, which can understand the things that they see. The problem is that our eyes do so much, so fast and then need such a very great deal of intelligence to interpret what they have done, that present-day computers cannot hope to compete.

▽ Machines which can read printed letters and numbers have been around for many years. Until recently they could only read specially designed characters, such as the OCRA-B numbers along the bottom of this cheque. Newer devices can read almost all types of printed letters.

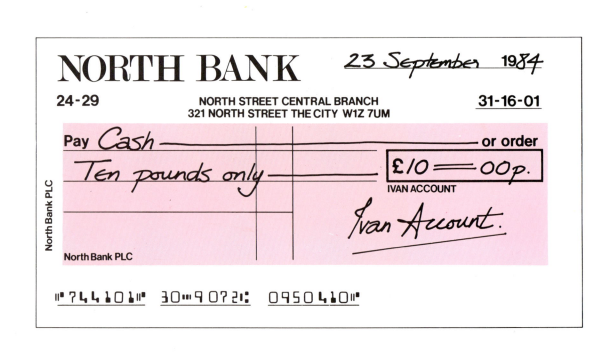

▷ This is a photograph of the spectacular M51 whirlpool galaxy. It was taken using a huge telescope and reveals everything that would be visible to us if we were to look through the same telescope ourselves. But there is more to be seen than meets the human eye.

The second picture (*below*) shows how computers can be used to bring out things which our senses miss. This coloured bar-chart shows where the light energy is highest in the galaxy photographed above.

▷ Using computers to add colours to pictures to make them more easily understood is called 'colour coding' or 'image enhancement'. It is a device used a great deal by astronomers.

Some stars and galaxies can only be detected by telescopes which are sensitive to X-rays, infra-red or ultra-violet light, or radio waves. The human eye cannot see any of these and so methods are needed to turn the images these telescopes form into images we can see.

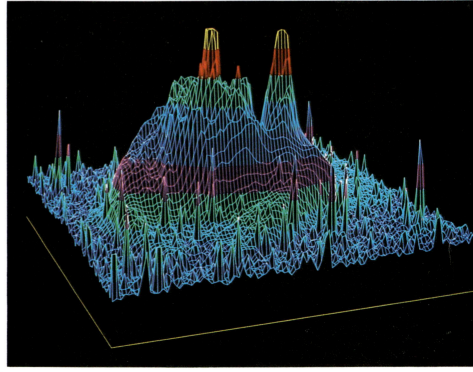

Touch

With your eyes closed, your mouth shut, and your ears and nose blocked, you are still able to discover a lot about the world outside you, purely through your sense of touch. Your whole skin is sensitive to touch, even inside your mouth and on your eyeballs.

Being sensitive to touch does not only mean that you are aware when something comes into contact with your skin. You can also often tell exactly what it is that is touching you. Your skin can feel the texture and temperature of objects which touch it and, if you move your hands over an object, you can usually tell what shape it is too. As with other senses, your understanding of touch can be improved with training and many blind people can use their fingers to read raised 'braille' writing or learn to recognize people's faces.

Touch is perhaps the most common sense of all and even microscopic, single-cell creatures will respond to physical contact. Insects and crustacea (crabs and shrimps) are often very sensitive to touch as this is often the first warning they have of the interest of a predator.

The importance of touch

For many mammals, touch is an important part of their social life and very many animals groom each other. For people touch is an essential part of our lives and babies who do not receive enough touching and cuddling may grow up emotionally disturbed and even physically small.

◁ This spider is sitting in its web waiting for a fly. It hooks its legs to the strands so that it can feel anything that touches the web. Flying insects which blunder into the web will stick to it and struggle violently to try to escape. This causes the web to vibrate and the spider can feel this vibration through its legs which are sensitive to the slightest movement. It can then follow the vibrations down to its struggling prey.

Sometimes you may see a spider go to the middle of its web after it has been away for a while and give the web a few short tugs. By doing this it makes the web vibrate. The spider feels the way its web vibrates, and can then find any insects which have become caught in the web while it was away.

▷ Different parts of your body are more sensitive to being touched than others. If we were able to make a man who was biggest in those parts where he was most sensitive to touch, he would probably look very much like this chap here.

We have a sense of touch because of nerve endings inside our skin. The skin on our finger-tips is crowded with them, but the skin on our backs has only a few. How sensitive any part of the body is depends on the number of nerve endings there.

▷ The mole is almost completely blind. It lives underground, coming up at night to feed on worms and other insects. One of the ways the mole has of finding its way around in the dark is by feeling its way with its very sensitive nose.

The end of the mole's nose is covered in short hairs and this helps to improve its sensitivity. Under the skin, a nerve ending is wrapped around each bristle, so that the very slightest movement of the hair can be felt.

Many other animals also use their noses for feeling for food. Some, including people, also have sensitive hairs. Others, like cats, can use their body fur to help them balance because it is so sensitive to movement.

Touch is a very short-range sense because it relies on actual physical contact with the animal that is being touched.

For this reason, some creatures have extended the range of their touch in some interesting ways. The most common way is to grow touch-sensitive antennae. These can be very long and elaborate and are found in insects, crustacea and some fish. Hairs on the body can also extend the space around an animal which it can feel and the same is true for tentacles, spines and long limbs.

▷ This lioness is licking her cubs. The cub enjoys the stroking of his mother's tongue and the mother enjoys the grooming of her baby. This affectionate act also serves the very valuable purpose of cleaning the cub. Many animals put touch to use in this way.

Touching each other can be very enjoyable for people as well as other animals. Cuddling and stroking are how people show other people that they like them or love them. Being cuddled regularly is very important for young children.

◁ This is a giant clam and like many creatures he uses touch to help him find food. He will sit at the bottom of the sea with his shell wide open until an unsuspecting fish settles on his tongue. Then he will snap shut, trapping his victim until he has eaten it.

Some sea-animals, such as jellyfish, dangle their tentacles in the water to sting and capture small creatures which touch them as they swim past. A few plants also use this method. The venus fly trap waits for insects to land on its sticky petals and then traps and eats them.

Hearing

Hearing is a sense which is only common in the more complex creatures. Insects make use of hearing when they communicate with each other, detecting the sounds with sensitive antennae or hollow cavities in their bodies. Other animals use their hearing to detect mating calls, warning calls and the approach of danger.

Sounds

Sounds are vibrations – which are tiny backward and forward movements. Vibrations travel easily through gases and liquids, such as air and water, but not very easily through solids. (A rabbit, however, may make use of these vibrations in its burrow [*see page 39*].) When a sound is made in air, the vibrations travel out in all directions. Ears are designed to collect these vibrations and to detect them. Because sound travels through water, our ears will work just as well underwater as in air. Next time you are having a bath, put your head under the water and listen.

▽ This frog has puffed up his throat ready to make his mating call. Other frogs around him will hear it and respond. For the frog, and for many other animals, sound is one of its main methods of communication.

Because we have such highly developed brains, people can use sound to represent ideas or meanings. Sounds which we use in this way, we call a language. People are clever enough to interpret very complicated spoken languages. Other animals also seem to use spoken languages, but usually they can convey only a few, very simple meanings to each other.

Exceptions to this rule may be whales and dolphins. These sea mammals communicate using very elaborate sequences of sounds which are at least as complicated as human speech. Whales and dolphins are highly intelligent and it is possible that they are able to understand very complicated messages.

△ Because hearing is such an important sense for most animals, a wide variety of ears exists in nature. Some of them – like those of the bat-eared fox – can be very spectacular. Ears serve to funnel sound down into the inner ear where they are detected by special nerve cells.

◁ People can hear a wide range of sound from very low to very high. Musicians make full use of this range. An orchestra can make sounds from the deep rumble of the kettle drum and double bass to the high squeak of the piccolo and violin.

△ These gophers, taking the air by their gopher hole, are always listening for the sounds of approaching danger. They are usually to be found close to the rims of their burrows and at the smallest sound they will take fright and dart into their holes to be out of harm's way.

For a small and defenceless animal like the gopher, good hearing is vital to give them a really early warning of predators.

Experiment!

Blindfolded, try to point to a friend who is humming quietly or clapping. The

start of a sound reveals where it is, so sudden sounds are easier to find.

Smell

High up, at the back of your nostrils are the cells which actually detect smells. They are arranged along a pair of shallow grooves and there are about 600,000 of them in all. They are kept clean and protected from the air passing them by a thin liquid called mucus which covers them. To detect a chemical passing through the nose it must first dissolve in this mucus layer. The sensory cells can then hold it briefly and send their messages to the brain.

Each different kind of animal has a different range of smells that it can detect. Even quite small creatures, like the locust which follows the scent of fresh grass, are sensitive to very small traces of scents. Dogs are well-known for their extreme sensitivity to smell, which is many, many times better than our own. But other animals, including many kinds of fish, have equally good noses.

▽ In the desert, in order to stay alive, an animal must find water. These camels are helped to survive by the fact that they can smell water. This seems strange to us but many animals can do this.

Have you ever wondered why your cat takes so much care to keep its fur clean? Many animals spend a great deal of their time cleaning themselves. This is because they are trying to remove their own odour. Not smelling strongly is important for animals as a protection against predators and to make sure that they do not give their presence away to animals they might be stalking. Ground-nesting birds do not line their nests (as tree-nesting birds do) so that their scent can be more easily absorbed by the earth.

Smell is very important to many animals because it is the signal for them to eat. Your cat or dog will rapidly devour a piece of liver placed in front of it but, if the liver has been washed thoroughly first to remove its smell, your pet may become very confused and appear not to be able to find the morsel it can see quite plainly.

Attacking the sense of smell

Octopusses, squids and cuttlefish squirt out ink into the water around them when attacked. This not only makes it difficult for their predators to see, but it contains a substance which dulls the sense of smell of the attacker.

Noses are usually found at the front of the head, close to the mouth. This is because of the close link between smelling and eating and smell and taste. The nile monitor, a snake, can detect smells with its long, forked tongue.

▷ This wild boar has been sniffing for food in the snow. When an animal's food is buried under the ground or by snow a sense of smell is often all that can locate it. All animals have a distinctive smell and as they move around they leave traces of this smell on the ground and on plants as they pass. Some animals can follow these scent trails to track down animals to eat.

People have often made use of dogs, which have a much better sense of smell than ours, to hunt for food or criminals. Dogs are still used by the police and the army to help them find illegal drugs or explosives. Even pigs have been used to help sniff out a kind of fungus called a truffle which grows under the ground.

△ The shark has poor eyesight and finds its prey with its extremely good sense of smell. People can smell things because human noses have nerve cells which detect tiny traces of chemicals which are floating in the air. Underwater, animals smell chemicals which are dissolved in the water. Sharks are said to be very fond of the smell of blood.

△ The proboscis monkey looks rather comical with its big red nose. An enormous variety of noses can be found, from the tiny holes in the beaks of birds to the great trunks of elephants, but all noses serve the same purpose – to draw air in to the sensitive cells inside.

▷ This lunar moth has very spectacular and beautiful antennae. The antennae of most insects are sensitive to smell in just the same way as our noses are. Lots of animals, including moths, can make smells which they use to communicate with other animals.

Taste

Taste is a rather unusual sense. It relies on nerve endings in the tongue as you might expect, but it also needs the sense of smell to work with it (as the experiment on *page 33* shows).

Taste buds

The nerve endings on the tongue (known as the taste buds) are mostly found around its edge, with many at the very back. They are sensitive to chemicals which dissolve in the saliva around them, sending their messages up to the brain. There are only four tastes that the tongue can detect. These are salt, sweet, bitter and sour.

Your mouth and nose are connected and scents from foods in your mouth pass from the back of the mouth to the nasal cavity (*see page 9*) where the smell is detected. The brain does not interpret these extra smell signals as smells, but somehow combines them with the taste signals. This produces the impression that we can detect, not four, but thousands of different tastes.

It is very difficult to study taste in people and in other animals and we still know less about it than we know about most of the other senses. Very many animals have a sense of taste and even single-celled amoeba respond to contact with food because of a chemical sensitivity to it. The earthworm is particularly unusual in that it is actually sensitive to taste on every bit of its body.

The chemistry of eating

Eating is a very complicated thing and involves the use of many senses together. These all act

▷ We taste by detecting the chemicals which make up our food. Some tastes, like salt, are simple chemicals but others, like meat and chocolate, are very complicated mixtures. We make some of these complicated tastes by mixing foods together when we cook.

A cook is very much like a chemist who mixes chemicals (ingredients) in special ways to produce a substance (food) which tastes and looks nice to eat. Cooking is a complex skill which has developed over thousands of years.

▷ This man is a wine taster. He has spent many years in training so that he can taste minute differences in wines that you and I would not be aware of. Some wine tasters become so skilled that they are able to say exactly where the grapes were grown that went into the wine.

Wine tasters are aware of the close connection between taste and smell and will always smell a wine as well as taste it. To taste the wine they will swill it about in their mouths so that it touches every part of their tongues. This ensures that all the different taste areas on the tongue come into contact with the wine.

◁ People are often guilty of thinking that other creatures must be more or less similar to themselves. Because our own sense of taste involves our mouth, we tend to assume it will be the same for other animals. This is not always true.

Flies do have a sense of taste in their mouths, but they can also taste with their feet. This is quite a common feature in insects.

with one another to determine the taste of the food.

The colour and appearance of food can alter the way we think it tastes. Blue fried eggs are reported to taste worse than normal ones, even though they have merely been coloured with a tasteless dye. For this reason good cooks around the world take great care to make their food look appetizing.

What affects our taste

The amount of hunger we are feeling also affects the taste of our food and someone who is very hungry will find the same food more tasty than when he is not. The smell of food is very important of course, especially to animals, and can easily affect the way we think it tastes.

▷ For insects who do not want to be eaten by other animals, it is useful to taste so horrible that nothing wants to eat them. Yet tasting nasty will not help if other animals have to eat you first to find out! So foul-tasting insects, like these moth larvae, have distinctive colouring to warn birds.

Many common insects, such as bees and wasps, also use their special colouring to warn birds not to eat them. It is lucky for the insects that birds have very good colour vision!

Experiment!

Blindfold a friend and hold his nose. Can he tell apple from potato?

Hold different foods under his nose while he eats pieces of potato. What can he taste?

This shows how taste is a sense which depends on the tongue as well as the nose.

Position sense

Every animal has a normal posture. A dog will stand with its four feet on the ground and its head facing away from its body; a fish will rest in the water with its belly down and its body parallel to the surface. Although the animal may be able to adopt any number of other positions, it will normally return to this one in the end.

To be able to keep itself in the positions it wants to adopt, the animal needs to be aware of where all its parts are, what its position is with respect to the ground or gravity or the river bank, which way is up and which way is front. If it makes any movements, it needs to know what its new position has become.

To get all this information, animals make use of a wide range of senses for feeling their own shape, for feeling their balance, and for comparing their position to the outside world.

△ A sense you might not always hear people mention is the sense of balance. Balancing involves knowing which way is up and knowing the positions of all the parts of your body.

◁ These astronauts working on a space shuttle do not need to worry about balance because there is no gravity. They do still have the problem of knowing which way round they are and where all their arms and legs are. They can get this information from senses in their muscles.

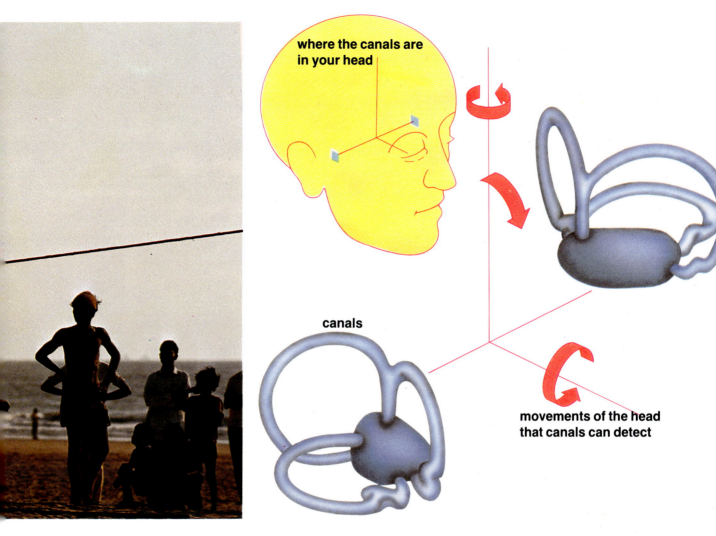

When we are just standing still we rely on two tiny sacs or cavities found in the inner ear called the sacculus and the utriculus. These are connected to the canals and all contain the same fluid.

Dizziness

A number of microscopic chalk particles are inside both the sacculus and the utriculus, and they rest on tiny hairs which are attached to the nerve cells. If the head tilts, the chalk particles press the hairs sideways and signals are sent to the brain. The fluid inside the sacculus and utriculus is constantly being spun around by tiny little hairs on the walls of the cavities. If we turn our heads too fast it upsets the spin of this fluid and we feel this as dizziness.

We feel the shape of our body because of nerve endings in the joints of our bones. When a joint moves, these cells signal the brain to tell it how much the joint moved. There are also nerve endings in the muscles and tendons which tell the brain how much the muscle is stretched.

△ We sense our own position with sense organs in our inner ears. Just behind each ear we have three tiny hoops filled with fluid. They are called canals and they are all at right-angles to each other.

When our head turns, the fluid in the canals turns and nerve endings in the fluid detect the movement and send a message to the brain. The brain works out from these messages which way round we are. Spinning around can confuse your position senses, so that when you stop you still feel you are spinning.

▷ Having a tail helps animals to balance. Not only can they steady themselves with it like this mouse is doing, but they can move it around to change their centre of gravity.

▽ This jellyfish manages to keep itself the right way up in the water because it can sense the pull of gravity. Gravity always pulls straight down, so feeling gravity can be very helpful for balance in water where you do not have the ground with which to compare your position.

Experiment!

Blindfolded, touch your nose. How did you know where it was?

Now try touching your ear lobe. Did you do any better?

Senses adapted for protection

To survive, an animal must eat. Yet, because many animals live by eating other animals, survival also means avoiding being eaten. In their efforts to stay away from hungry predators, animals have some powerful allies: their own senses. They can also make use of the senses of other animals by, for instance, using protective colouring. Many animals use camouflage but some have patterning which repels their predators. Some moths, for example, have two large dots on their wings which look like eyes and scare off birds.

Senses help protect animals by warning them when danger threatens. The best defence any animal has against its predators is to run away to safety before the predator even notices it. The most useful senses for this are sight, hearing and smell because they can give long-range warnings, but other senses are often used as well. A mole will eat as many as 300 earthworms a day, so it is in the worm's interest to know when a mole is near. Worms can feel the vibrations made by the burrowing of moles and will dig themselves out of the ground when they do, lest they are caught under the surface and eaten.

▽ Grazing animals like these zebra are easy prey for fast, powerful hunters like the lion. Zebra live out in the open and they are not fierce or strong. Their only hope of survival is to have an early enough warning of the approaching menace to run away before it is too late. Their senses of smell and hearing can provide this warning.

Hunting animals, such as lions, stalk their prey very quietly so as not to be heard.

It is not only predators which threaten the lives of animals. There are also dangers in their natural environment. Amphibians, such as frogs and newts, which spend too much time out of water, may suffer because their skin dries up. They therefore have senses in their skin which warn them of the need to find water.

Hibernation

Winter hibernations save many animals from the cold weather when they would find it very difficult to find food and would struggle to move around in the snow. Hibernation is often triggered, not by temperature, but by the shortening of the days.

The third 'eye'

In all vertebrate animals (those with spines, such as fish, birds, and mammals) there is a third 'eye' called the pineal eye which is located at the top of the brain. In the distant past this may have been a fully functioning pair of eyes in its own right, but now it serves to regulate processes such as sleep and activity. It is sensitive in some animals to sunlight and may be the sense which regulates hibernation.

◁ The sense of smell of the animals which prey on it works to the skunk's advantage because its main defence against attack is to release a foul-smelling vapour which drives the attacker away. Upsetting another animal's senses is one way that animals can protect themselves.

▷ The rabbit uses every sense it can to help to protect itself from its many predators. Very often while it is eating it will sit up on its hind legs to sniff the air, listen and watch for signs of danger. Its feet are especially sensitive and can feel the vibrations that other animals make when they tread on the ground.

▽ These sea-anemones catch small sea creatures in their lovely, waving tentacles. If a larger creature were to touch these tentacles though, the anemone would pull them down in a flash into the safety of the hard shell at its base.

Experiment!

Find a sleeping cat and click your fingers a few feet away.

Its ears will turn to point towards you. You may be a danger!

Senses adapted for navigation

Finding your way about your house, your town, or the world, is called navigation. The way you do it most of the time is probably by learning the route you must take; remembering the names of roads, the landmarks along the way and the sequence of left and right turnings.

This is true for other animals too, who make small, frequent journeys. Some creatures, like homing pigeons, make journeys which are far too long for them to have memorized or, like the salmon, can migrate thousands of kilometres to places they have never been before. They always return to the same river.

Migrating animals

Migrating animals have puzzled us for centuries but some of the mystery is beginning to be unravelled. Many birds and fish are now believed to make use of a magnetic sense, while fish may also use water currents and a memory of tiny traces of smells in the oceans to find their way. Birds, it is believed, navigate by the Sun and stars, judging their position by accurate internal 'clocks' as seamen used to do.

△ Homing pigeons can find their way home from such great distances because they can feel the Earth's magnetic field.

▽ Bats fly at night. They make lots of very fast squeaking sounds which bounce back from things around them so they can work out where they are.

△ The search for food takes many animals on long journeys each year. Sometimes they travel hundreds or even thousands of kilometres. Finding their way on these migrations often requires special senses that we do not have.

The monarch butterfly has a spectacular migration when huge flocks travel great distances across America. The monarchs, like other animals with compound eyes, can sense a property of sunlight called polarization and use this to guide them on their long travels. Bees use polarization to guide them to food.

▷ Fish use a special sense of touch to help them navigate. They have channels in the sides of their bodies with which they can feel the direction of the currents in the water. This is a good example of how an animal's senses make the most of the information available.

▽ When ants go out to forage for food they leave scent trails which they can follow to find their way home.

Bees were among the first animals to be shown to have a magnetic sense of direction. They also have some interesting aids to navigation. Some of these methods have been helpful to us.

On each of the sides of a bee's compound eyes is a tiny hair. These hairs feel the wind direction as the bee is flying so that she can take this into account and correct her course. Bees, like many other flying insects, also have their own gyroscopes. These take the form of tiny wings set behind the large true wings. They are connected to nerve endings at their base and any twisting or turning of the bee in flight stretches these nerve endings and sends signals to the bee's primitive brain.

Experiment!

Choose an object, then close your eyes and point to it. How did you do?

Close your eyes, turn around twice and try again. Better or worse?

Machine senses in navigation

It is difficult for people to find their way around in places that they are not familiar with. Unlike many other animals, we have no special sensory apparatus to help us navigate at all. To compensate for this we have developed a large variety of artificial senses, especially for navigating at sea, where there are no landmarks, and in the air, where the land may be out of sight.

From birds to radar

One of the earliest tricks used by seamen was to take along a supply of migrant birds. When the men needed to know the direction, they released one of the birds which would always fly off in a known direction. The ship's compass finally made this unnecessary. Later, sensing equipment included methods for taking bearings from radio beacons (which may be in orbit these days) and radar. Radio beacons and radar are often used for aircraft navigation. Since the Second World War, aircraft have used a sensor called the radio altimeter which bounces radio waves off the ground to let the pilot know how high the aircraft is.

▽ Very often we give our machines senses which add to or extend our own. To be able to fly an aeroplane the pilot must know how much it is tilted. When he cannot see the ground, this becomes extremely difficult, so he relies on a mechanical position sense provided by a device called a gyroscope.

The gyroscope always stays at the same angle no matter how much the aircraft tilts. The angle of the aircraft therefore can be compared to the angle of the gyroscope.

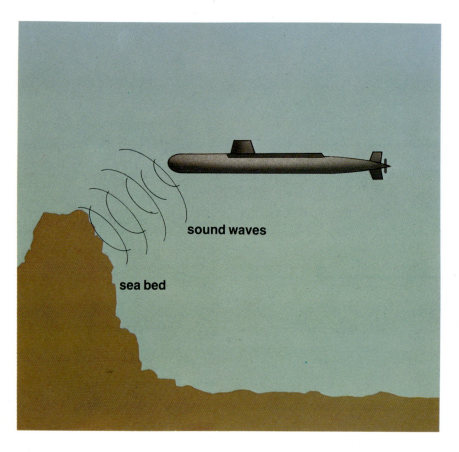

◁ Under the water, submarines use sonar to help them navigate. Sonar works by sending high-pitched sounds out into the water and then listening for the echoes.

Sound travels in water and air as waves. If these waves hit a solid object they bounce back. Sensitive microphones in the sonar equipment pick up the reflected sounds. The time it takes the echo to come back tells the sonar operator how far away the object is. By measuring the distance to the object at different times as the submarine moves along, the position of the object can also be calculated.

▷ The Earth is magnetic. Just like a bar magnet it has a North and South pole.

Thousands of years ago, the Chinese discovered that certain magnetic ores will, if they are allowed to turn freely, always line themselves up with the Earth's magnetic poles. Iron magnets can also 'feel' the Earth's magnetic field in this way and for centuries we have used this knowledge to make compasses to help us to find our way.

Artificial senses used for human navigation have certainly made life easier for seamen and aviators. The same technology which guides ships and planes is now also being developed to guide mobile robots in factories.

One of the simplest ways of helping a robot to find its way between rows of machines and around huge warehouses is to place beacons around the building, just like the radio beacons that aircraft use.

These beacons can transmit light, radio or ultrasound signals which the robot must be able to sense. If the robot knows the positions of the beacons, the robot can be sure of being able to work out its own position.

Keeping the traffic moving

A new development in some countries is the placing of radio transmitters along the road edge. Cars equipped with radio receivers can tune in to these broadcasts to hear warnings of hazards and route changes ahead as well as weather-forecasts.

Putting sensors beside traffic signals can help traffic move around towns. The effects of different kinds of vehicles passing through an electric field can be detected and used to switch the traffic lights. In this way buses or emergency services can be given a clear passage around town. In Japan, a more elaborate scheme is being tested.

▷ This naval frigate is bristling with all kinds of artificial senses including sonar, lasers, infra-red detectors, and radio. In particular, it has a great many radar antennae. Radar works by bouncing a radio beam off surrounding objects and then sensing the echo.

Radar is a vital aid to navigation at sea. It can penetrate farther than human eyes even in mists and fog which we would not be able to see through. It can also help keep ships clear of the coast and shallow waters.

Senses for communication

There is no doubt that people are the most communicative animals in the world. Other animals may talk as much as we do, particularly dolphins and whales, but none have written or pictorial communication as well. While we use our enormous ability for communication to pass very complicated ideas and knowledge between ourselves, most other animals do an excellent job.

The role of the senses in communication is to be the receivers for the incoming signals. This means that to understand what one creature is trying to communicate, the other creature must have a sense that can detect the message that the first is trying to send.

The deaf and the blind

People who lose one or more of their senses, usually lose some part of their communication with the world. This is not always lost for good though because people have been very clever in finding ways to make up for the loss. Blind people may learn to read through their sense of touch with the aid of Braille books; deaf people may still be able to join in with spoken conversations by learning the art of lip-reading or by using sign language. Blind and deaf people may still be able to follow a conversation by touching the lips of the speaker or by using a sign langauge, touching the palm of the hand.

Fish and communication

There are as many ways of communicating in nature as there are senses. Animals make use of almost all of them, including electric fields, flickering light and body postures. It is not often realized that fish communicate to quite a degree by using sounds. Fish have good hearing and water is a good conductor of sound waves. They make sounds in a number of ways, often by filling a bladder with air and blowing it out to make rasping sounds.

◁ All around the elephant fish is a tiny electric current which passes through the water. It uses slight changes in this electric field to communicate with other elephant fish who can also feel the current.

Some fish, like electric eels, generate strong electric current with which they are able to stun other fish. But these fish are not sensitive to weak electric current as the elephant fish is.

◁ This lion is marking his territory. You may have seen a dog or cat doing this. The scent he is spraying is made by special scent glands and warns other lions that they are trespassing on land that he has claimed. The amount of territory an animal can claim will depend on how big and strong he is.

▷ Moths use their sight and smell to communicate with other moths. They release scents to say when they are ready to mate and the rate at which they flap their wings indicates which sex they are. Moths can see very fast flickering where we would seen only a blur.

▷ This girl is not saying a word and yet you still know exactly what she thinks about the crab she is holding! She tells you with her expression and the positions of her hands and her body. It is what you can see rather than what you can hear which conveys the message.

Using your body and face to communicate is called 'body language' and many animals make use of it. Animals such as dogs can start or end a fight by adopting aggressive or submissive postures. Animals, particularly birds, may also entice a mate with the right actions or poses.

◁ Senses give animals an awareness of what is happening in the world. They need to know where to find food, where danger lies, and where to find safety, pleasure, and companions. But senses also serve to let animals know about other animals.

Most animals, especially people, use languages to communicate their emotions and desires. A language can be a set of words, like our own, but it can also be any set of signs an animal can make that another can detect and understand. This signpost is a kind of language.

Extending human senses

An animal's senses protect it by informing it about dangers which may threaten. They also help it to survive by allowing it to communicate with its fellows and to find food. Like every other animal, people have used the full range of their senses in all these ways, but we have always felt the need to see farther, to hear more, to go beyond the limits of our own senses.

Methods from the past

In the past, people have made good use of animals as extensions of their own senses. Dogs have been trained to sniff for us, following scent trails or finding substances our own noses cannot detect. Seamen on long voyages would sometimes release birds to guide them to land. If there was land nearby, the bird would fly straight towards it. If not, it would circle the ship. In the days when hawking was a common sport, the hawker could take a caged songbird along with him to help him spot his hawk high in the air. The bird's keen eyesight would locate the hawk and it would then show by cowering and fearful glances where to look for the hawk.

Sometimes our own senses are not sensitive enough. Coal mining used to be dangerous because of poisonous gases which seep out of the rock. People cannot smell these gases, so miners used to take caged canaries with them into the mines. If a canary died, the miners would know that gas was about.

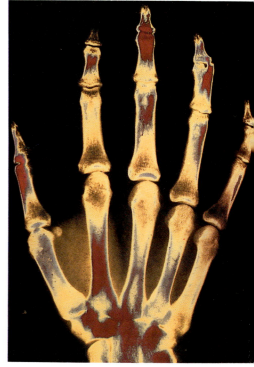

△ X-rays are a kind of radiation which passes easily through our flesh but less easily through bones. If X-rays are shone through a hand like this and onto a photographic plate, they leave an image of the bones inside the hand.

This allows doctors to look inside us to see things which their own senses cannot detect.

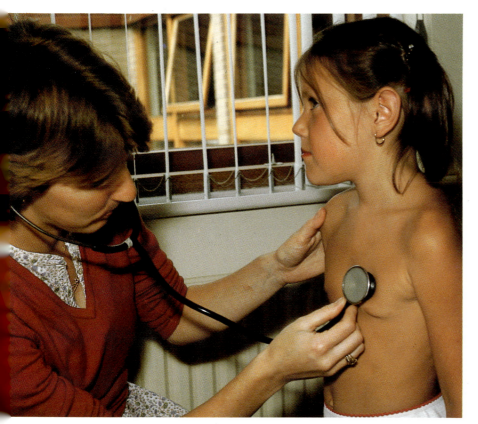

◁ Our bodies make several sounds which can tell a doctor something about our health. The heart beats as its muscles contract, air moves through the narrow passages in our lungs and even our blood makes a sound as it moves through our veins and arteries.

The tiny differences in these sounds, which tell the doctor we are ill, are too small for our ears to detect without help.

Many devices which we take for granted in our everyday life are extensions of our natural senses. The telephone and the radio allow us to hear people's voices and other sounds over thousands of kilometres. Similarly, television can transmit visual images around the world. Recent space explorations have sent television cameras to the outer planets to send back pictures.

The benefit to human communication and to science is tremendous. The most spectacular example must be the day that the American President spoke on the telephone to astronauts who were on the Moon.

▽ A simple telescope is a tube with a lens at both ends; one to capture and concentrate the light and one to focus it for the eye.

Modern telescopes, like the one used to take this photograph, enable us to see millions of stars unknown to the ancient astronomers.

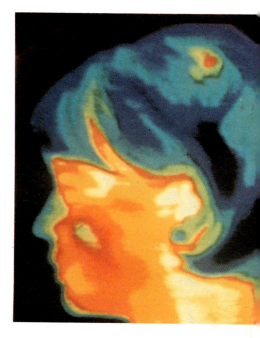

△ All around us there is a hidden universe of life so small we do not see it. This fascinating picture is of the tongue of a moth. There are a million nerve cells in our eyes, but we are still unable to see such fine detail. Magnifying lenses and microscopes enlarge that detail for us and make it visible.

△ Harmful growths under the skin change the temperature of the skin a tiny amount which we would not be able to detect with our own senses.

This photograph was taken with a camera using a special infra-red film which is sensitive only to heat and not visible light. It can let a doctor see minute differences in skin temperature.

Experiment!

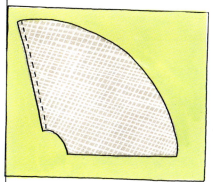

Improve your own hearing! Draw this shape on some card.

Cut it out, roll it up into a cone and stick the edge down. Your cone is like a big ear.

It captures the sound from one direction and channels it to your ear.

Machine senses for survival

Survival is the main purpose of all animals. It is not surprising then that we have armed ourselves with a battery of artificial senses to help us to achieve this. Fire alarms are one example of the use of artificial senses to save lives. These consist of a set of electronic sensors in the rooms of a building, each of which sends its signals to a central control unit. This unit can sound alarms and send a call to the fire brigade. The detectors in a fire alarm can sense increase in temperature, the presence of smoke, or the light given off by a fire.

Medical techniques

It is sometimes a matter of life and death to be able to detect what our unaided senses would miss. Many illnesses need special sensing equipment to spot them and doctors today can see inside the body in several ways. These include X-rays and infra-red. The tiny electric currents generated by our brains can also be detected using EEG machines and can tell doctors about brain damage.

▽ These huge white domes are an eerie sight out on the lonely English moors. Inside them are massive radar dishes which watch the sky constantly for signs of attack by hostile countries. Their job is to give the country's armed forces an early warning of attack.

Radar is an ideal 'sense' for this. Like eyesight, it relies on reflected radiation but uses radio waves instead of light. This means that radar can be relied on to 'see' farther than we can.

▷ These soldiers are looking for buried mines. The devices they are using generate a small electric field around the hoop at the bottom. They can then detect the presence of metal which disturbs this electric field. The Army calls this job 'mine sweeping'. The same metal-detecting equipment has recently become popular for finding buried coins and other metal treasures.

▷ Most weather-forecasting these days is done on the basis of weather satellite pictures like this. Being able to see the Earth from space can give us warning of bad weather on its way and can sometimes save lives. The swirling cloud pattern in this photograph is a dying storm – but it might just as easily have been a hurricane, in which case the people living in its path could have been warned or evacuated.

Surveillance from space can also show the movement of troops, ships or the launching of missiles and can warn countries of possible attack from its enemies. That is why some countries have orbiting 'spy' satellites.

◁ This Geiger counter senses radioactivity. Inside it is a tube carrying a large electric charge. When radioactive particles enter the tube they cause a spark. The spark is detected and amplified to produce a click on a loudspeaker. The more radiation there is about, the faster the Geiger counter will click.

Some kinds of nuclear radiation are very dangerous and in large doses can even kill people. Dangerous levels of radioactivity are very rare in nature and so we and other animals have not developed the ability to detect radiation with our own senses. Because of this inability, the Geiger counter is a vital piece of safety equipment for people who work with nuclear power.

Experiment!

Make a web of black cotton over your vegetable patch to protect it.

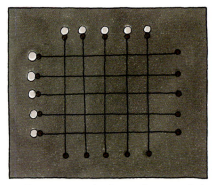

Fasten each thread to a stick and tie a tin can with a few pebbles in it to the other end.

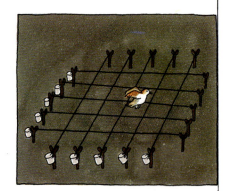

The birds will not see the threads and will rattle the cans when they touch them.

Five other senses

Although people usually say that we have five senses, the truth is far more complicated. We have already seen that we also have a position sense, which includes our sense of balance and several movement senses. Even the familiar senses are more complicated than they seem. Taste only works together with smell, the rods and cones in our eyes mean that we see in black and white as well as colour, and touch is a mixture of touch, heat, cold, and pain.

As well as these six, complicated senses, we have a wide selection of others. We can sense the chemistry of our blood in several ways to know when we are tired or aroused or short of breath. We can also feel our bladder and our bowel motions.

Fooling the brain

Our sense organs are intended to send signals to the brain only in response to particular kinds of stimulation, but they can also be made to sense other things.

Close your eyes and press gently on the side of one eye gently with a finger. You will 'see' a round shape appear at the opposite side of the eye. The pressure you are making inside your eye is causing the cells of the retina to send off signals. This fools your brain into thinking that they have detected some light.

▷ When your stomach is full of food it is big and when it is empty it is small. You feel hunger mainly because you can sense the size of your stomach. This is due to nerve endings in your stomach wall which can sense how much it is being stretched. It is possible that some people become very fat because this sense does not work properly. They cannot feel when their stomachs are full and so cannot tell when to stop eating.

The amount of chewing and swallowing you do while eating affects how full you feel. You are also sensing the amount of sugar in your blood and in your liver. Hunger also depends on your eating habits, food preferences, mood, the taste and even the appearance of your food.

A sense of time

A very interesting sense that people and animals seem to possess is a sense of time. Many animals go through a daily routine which is very precisely timed. The lugworm, which lives in a U-shaped burrow on sandy beaches, comes to the top of its burrow every 40 minutes to squirt out its worm-cast and every seven minutes it extends a tube from its head to suck in sand for feeding.

Many other animals are equally punctual and control such behaviours as eating and sleeping by regular internal 'clocks'. People too can sense the passage of time quite accurately.

◁ Pain is a sense which is very much like the sense of touch. We feel pain through special pain cells in our skin. When these cells are moved they send signals to the brain which we feel as pain. Some pain cells are not very sensitive but some, like those in your eyes, need only the slightest touch to hurt you.

◁ How do you know when you are thirsty? When you are thirsty it is because your body needs water. You must have water to live, so your body has a set of nerve cells inside it which can feel how much water is in the blood which flows around them. When the water level is low, they signal the brain and you begin to feel all the sensations that tell you you are thirsty.

When you drink, the amount of liquid you swallow is also detected and this tells you when it is time to stop drinking.

People and other animals can also sense heat. Measuring the heat inside as well as outside our bodies is a very important job for our senses. Like other mammals, we need to keep our bodies at the right temperature or else we can become ill and die. To help us, our bodies generate their own heat.

Sweating and goose bumps

We have nerve endings which feel the temperature of our blood. If they show that we are too hot our skin may redden and we might start to sweat. These are both ways ways of cooling down. If we are too cold, we will shiver and our hair muscles will tense (goose bumps).

▷ Pit vipers get their name from the pits or depressions at the front of their heads above the nostrils. These have membranes of skin stretched across them which are full of nerve cells sensitive to heat.

In the pits of the rattle snake there are as many heat-sensitive cells as there are in the whole skin. This gives them what amounts to two eyes for seeing heat.

In fact the pit vipers rely far more on their pits for detecting the small animals they feed on than they do their eyes. A rattle snake, with tape over its pits but its eyes uncovered, will ignore mice placed in front of it. Another, one with its eyes blindfolded but with its pits clear, will quickly catch and eat the mice.

Because there are two pits, the vipers can use them in very much the same way as we use our eyes to judge distances and sizes. By moving its head from side to side, the snake can tell how big the animal in front of it is.

Beyond human senses

There are many ways in which the senses of animals go beyond human senses. Although our senses each have a good range, other animals have senses which detect things that we miss.

A large number of animals have a far superior sense of smell. Dogs are the best example of this and they use their sense of smell for identifying one another and for finding their way around. Fish too have an excellent sense of smell. Many birds see finer detail than we do and insects can see a kind of light which we cannot. Some bats are very sensitive to heat on their bodies and, while hanging asleep, will react to the heat from a person nearby.

Hearing and taste

Many animals also have a far better sense of hearing than ours. Some hear sounds too high for our ears to detect; some hear sounds too low; and some, like dogs and cats, are able to hear sounds too quiet for us to notice. It is more difficult to tell which animals have a greater sense of taste than ours, but some, such as flies and rats, are known to have a greater sensitivity to certain tastes.

Other animals do not only go beyond human senses by detecting more of the same things that we can. They also detect things which we have no senses for at all.

Insects

Sand fleas, like most insects, can detect the polarity of light. This is a good guide to where the Sun is (even when it is behind clouds) and they use it to orientate themselves so they can find the sea. Insects also hear in a slightly different way to us, detecting the actual movement of the air caused by a sound rather than the pressure waves. This means they can judge the direction from which a sound came much more accurately.

Many insects also have humidity detectors. The human louse and the locust have them on their antennae and use them to find their way.

Birds

The swift and the swallow have an interesting addition to their eyes. They have two foveas in each eye instead of just one like us. This means that each separate eye can judge depth at close distances.

◁ These migrating birds can feel the magnetic field which is around the Earth. This sense acts like a compass for them and they can find their way across great distances.

This may be the way that all migrating birds, as well as some fish, navigate. We know that certain microscopic creatures use a magnetic sense to find their way about.

▷ Many animals can actually sense things which we do not. This owl can see a kind of light called infra-red which we can only just detect. Things which are warm give off infra-red light, so the owl can see and hunt mice and other small animals even when it is so dark that we cannot see at all.

Close your eyes tightly in a dark room and you may see a very faint, dark red colour. This is because your eyes are seeing the heat from your own body.

◁ The grasshopper communicates using a series of chirrupping sounds which it makes by rubbing its hind legs together. Some of these sounds are ultrasonic, which means they are too high for us to hear. Dogs can also hear ultrasonic sounds.

△ Compound eyes, like this fly has, are sensitive to a kind of light which we cannot see. Many flowers glow in ultra-violet light and so remain visible at dusk to the insects which pollinate them.

◁ Whales are intelligent animals and have a complicated language of sounds with which they communicate. Some of the sounds they use are subsonic, which means that they are too low for people to hear.

Some useful machines

All around us in our everyday lives we are seeing and using machines which have some simple sensory ability built into them. The more that a machine can know and do for itself, the more it leaves people free to do other things beside control it.

Part of the constant effort to make our machines more useful has been to give them more ways of knowing about the world around them as it affects their particular tasks.

Senses and cars

We have given cars the sensors necessary to check their own fuel levels and we have given vending machines the ability to tell whether they have sold out of their stock and whether their money collecting box is full. These 'senses' are all simple mechanical or electrical devices, but this does not make them very different from natural sensing equipment. The real difference between machine senses and natural senses is in the interpretation of the signals they send off. Unfortunately, the 'brains' of our machines are still very primitive.

△ Many machine senses are rather like our own. Imagine the trouble you might have if you did not know when your stomach was full or empty.

Inside a vacuum cleaner is a bag which collects the dust it has sucked up. When the bag is full, the user cannot usually tell without opening the cleaner to see. The vacuum cleaner in the picture can sense when its bag is full and will then tell the user.

◁ The keypad standing on top of this television can send signals from several yards away which the TV can detect and interpret as instructions to change channel.

The videotape recorder under the TV is also sensitive to these signals and can be controlled by a keypad. The signals are usually ultra-sound which we cannot hear.

One of the most useful artificial sensors is the thermostat. This is a device that is sensitive to temperature and can be found in kettles, cookers and central heating systems. The thermostat is set to a particular temperature and works as a switch.

When the temperature goes above the set temperature, the thermostat switches off the heating. With the heating off, the temperature falls, and when it has fallen below the set temperature, the thermostat will switch the heating back on again. In this way a constant temperature can be maintained.

△ The machines we use are becoming more and more sophisticated and many now have built-in computers. They are also gaining a whole range of senses.

Overloading a washing machine can damage the motor and the drum. This washing machine can tell when it has been overloaded and will not work until the load has been reduced. The 'sense' is based on a simple mechanical detector. It is no different in principle to the muscle sense in your limbs, which saves you from pulling or pushing too hard.

◁ This designer is using a computer to help him with his work. A computer's main way of sensing the world around it is its keyboard, but many other sensing devices can be attached. This one has a position-sensing device called a 'mouse' (*bottom right*) which tells the computer where it is on the desk.

△ Sonar is a sense which can tell animals how far away an object is. Sonar is also used on ships and submarines to locate objects which are under water.

This camera uses a sonar system to focus itself automatically. Ultra-sound signals are bounced off objects in front of the camera and detected by a microphone under the lens. The micro-electronic 'brain' inside the camera can work out the distance that the reflected sounds have travelled. A small electric motor then turns the lens to change its focus.

There's more to this...

Three blind men were asked to describe an elephant.
'It is a big, fat snake,' said the first.
'It is four thick pillars, like tree trunks,' said the second.
'It is long and thin, like a piece of string,' said the third.
Which one was right? None of them, of course, but in a way they all were. Being blind, they could not see the whole elephant and had each felt only a part of it. The first had felt its trunk, the second its legs, and the third its tail. If no one told these men about what an elephant looks like, they could each, for all their lives, have a different belief about what an elephant is!

Yet, even with eyesight, can we be sure that we know what an elephant is really like? After all, we have seen that many other creatures could have a different view of an elephant altogether. Think about what it might look like to a fly's compound eye with its ultra-violet vision, or to an owl with its infra-red vision.

Think of how it would smell to a dog and how it would feel to a mole's sensitive nose. What might an elephant seem like to a bat with sonar? There are radiations that would pass straight through an elephant. If we built robots to detect these radiations we would find that elephants seemed invisible to them!

Our senses give us a way of knowing about the world, but it is not the only way. And the world we know may be very different from the worlds of other creatures.

Index

Aircraft 43
Antennae 24, 30
Ants 41
Astronauts 33

Baboon 18
Balance 7, 33, 34, 35
Bat-eared fox 26
Blindness 23, 47
Body language 48
Braille 47
Brain 4, 6, 10, 12, 34, 55
Butterflies 40
Buzzard 16

Camels 28
Cameras 19, 63
Camouflage 13, 36, 37
Canals 34
Cats 16, 29
Chameleon 13
Chemicals 8, 15, 30
Cheques 20
Colour coding 21
Compass 44
Computers 6, 21, 62
Cones 12
Cooking 31
Cornea 10

Dizziness 29
Dogs 28, 29

Ear 4, 7, 33, 34, 35, 51
EEG machines 52
Elephant fish 47
Eyes 5, 10, 16, 18, 21
  compound 17, 40, 60
  simple 17
Eyesight 16, 17, 18, 59

Fish 41
Frogs 18, 25

Geiger counter 54
Gophers 26

Grasshoppers 26
Gyroscope 42

Hair 23, 24
Hearing 4, 7, 25, 26, 27, 51
Housefly 17, 32
Hunger 55, 56, 57

Infra-red light 19, 21, 45, 51, 59
Iris 5

Jellyfish 35

Languages 47, 48
Larvae 33
Laser 45
Lens 10, 11, 17
Lions 24, 36, 46, 47
Long-sightedness 11

Magnetic field 39, 30, 41, 44, 58
Microscopes 51
Migration 39, 40, 58
Mine-sweeping 53
Monkeys 18, 30
Moths 30, 47, 51
Music 26

Navigation 39, 40, 41, 42, 43, 44
Nerve endings 23
Nerve fibres 6
Nostrils 28

Octopus 16, 29
Optical illusions 13, 14, 15
Optic nerve 10

Pain 56
Photography 50, 51, 53, 63
Position sense 9
Pupil 5

Radar 45, 52
Radio 43, 44, 52

Retina 10, 12
Robots 19, 20, 43
Rods 12

Sacculus 29
Saliva 8, 31
Scent trails 41
Sea-anemones 38
Shark 30
Short-sightedness 11
Skunk 33
Smell 5, 28, 29, 30, 36, 37, 38
Snakes 16, 57
Sonar 44, 45, 63
Sound 25, 26, 27, 44
Space 33, 53
Spiders 17, 22
Submarines 44
Survival 36, 37, 38

Taste 5, 31, 32, 33, 35
  buds 31
Telescopes 21, 50
Television 50, 61
Temperature 57
Tentacles 24
Thermostat 62
Thirst 56
Tongues 32
Touch 4, 23, 24
Traffic signals 43

Utriculus 29

Vacuum cleaners 61
Venus fly trap 24

Washing machines 62
Weather-forecasting 53
Whales 60
Whirlpool galaxy 21
Wine-tasting 32

X-rays 21, 49, 52

Zebra 36